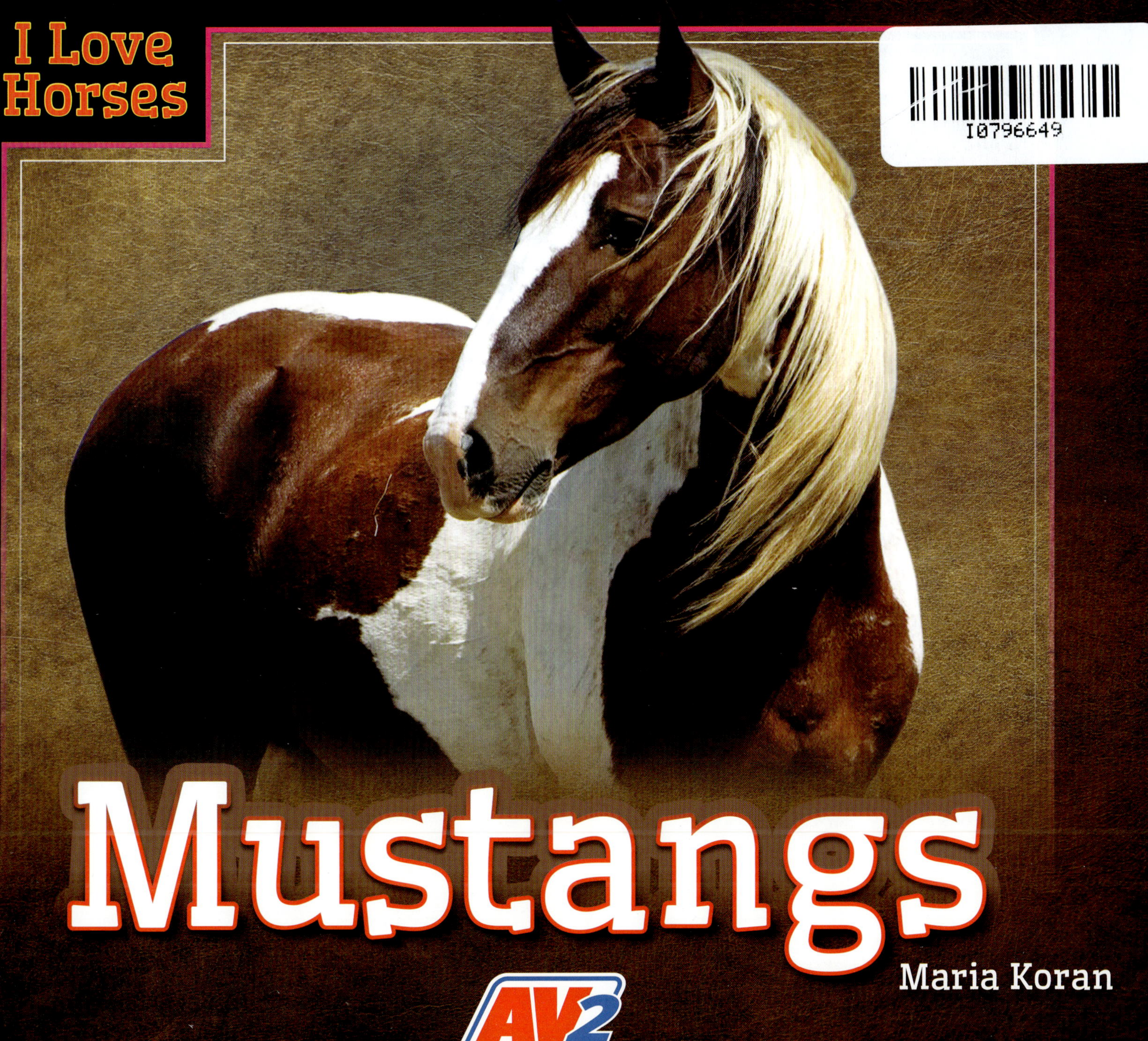

Mustangs

Maria Koran

AV2

Step 1
Go to **www.av2books.com**

Step 2
Enter this unique code
YPTGEFEA4

Step 3
Explore your interactive eBook!

AV2
I Love Horses
Mustangs
Start!

AV2 is optimized for use on any device

Your interactive eBook comes with...

Audio
Listen to the entire book read aloud

Videos
Watch informative video clips

Weblinks
Gain additional information for research

Try This!
Complete activities and hands-on experiments

Key Words
Study vocabulary, and complete a matching word activity

Quizzes
Test your knowledge

Slideshows
View images and captions

View new titles and product videos at www.av2books.com

Mustangs

CONTENTS

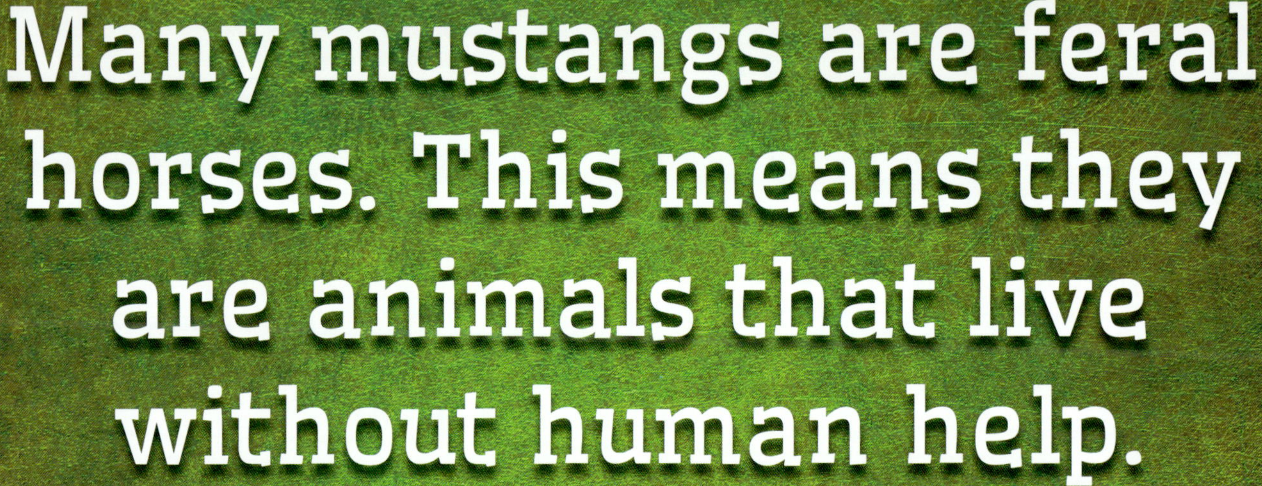

Many mustangs are feral horses. This means they are animals that live without human help.

Most feral mustangs in the United States live in Nevada.

Mustangs come from a mix of different horses.

Mustangs are usually small. They have strong bodies and legs.

Mustangs can live to be up to 40 years old.

Mustangs come in many colors. They can be brown, white, black, or a mix. Many mustangs have patches or spots.

Many mustangs are not used to people. It takes time to earn their trust.

Mustangs that trust people are friendly horses.

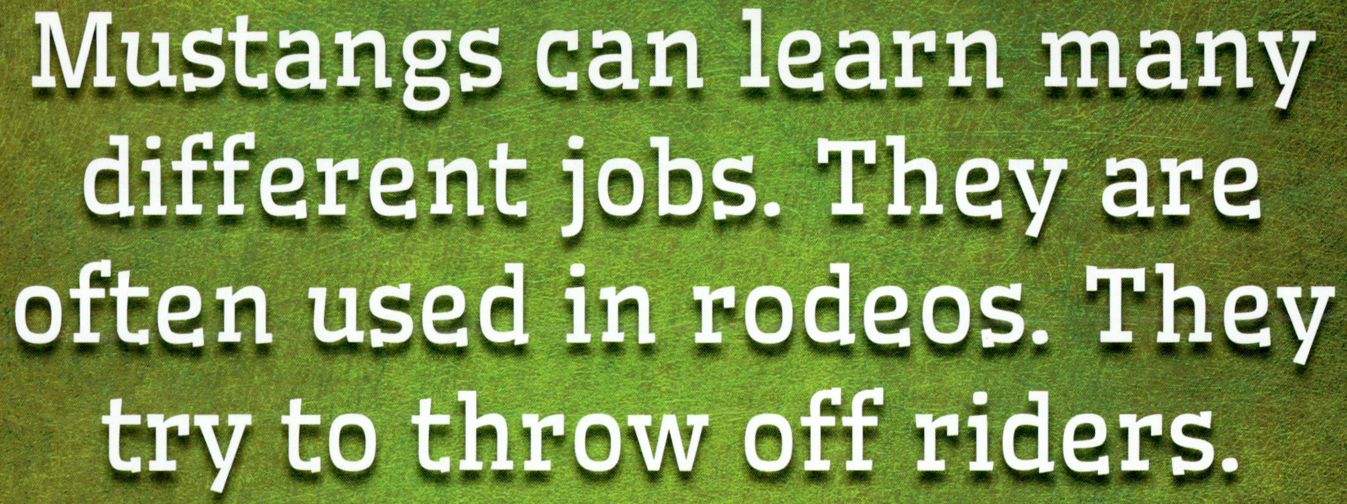

Mustangs can learn many different jobs. They are often used in rodeos. They try to throw off riders.

Native Americans started working with mustangs about 400 years ago.

In nature, mustangs live in a group called a herd.

Young mustangs can run right after they are born.

Young mustangs stay with a herd for up to two years.

Mustangs came from European horses. These horses were brought to America many years ago.

Over time, some horses ran away. They became feral.

Frederic Remington.

Mustangs ate the same food as cows. Some people wanted to get rid of them.

Other people tried to help mustangs. They gave these horses a space of their own.

Mustangs are an important part of American history.

Today, they run free on millions of acres of land in the United States.

Which of
these pictures
show mustangs?

KEY WORDS

Research has shown that as much as 65 percent of all written material published in English is made up of 300 words. These 300 words cannot be taught using pictures or learned by sounding them out. They must be recognized by sight. This book contains 69 common sight words to help young readers improve their reading fluency and comprehension. This book also teaches young readers several important content words, such as proper nouns. These words are paired with pictures to aid in learning and improve understanding.

Page	Sight Words First Appearance
4	animals, are, help, in, live, many, means, most, that, the, they, this, without
7	a, and, be, big, can, come, different, from, have, of, old, small, to, up, years
8	or, white
11	it, not, people, takes, their, time
12	about, for, learn, off, often, started, try, with
15	after, group, right, run, two, young
16	away, came, over, some, these, were
18	as, food, get, same, them
19	gave, other, own
21	an, important, land, on, part

Page	Content Words First Appearance
4	horses, human, mustangs, Nevada, United States
7	bodies, legs
8	colors, patches, spots
11	trust
12	jobs, Native Americans, riders, rodeos
15	herd, nature
18	cows
19	space
21	acres, history, United States

Published by AV2
350 5th Avenue, 59th Floor New York, NY 10118
Website: www.av2books.com

Library of Congress Control Number: 2019955098

ISBN 978-1-7911-1959-1 (hardcover)
ISBN 978-1-7911-1960-7 (softcover)
ISBN 978-1-7911-1961-4 (multi-user eBook)
ISBN 978-1-7911-1962-1 (single-user eBook)

Printed in Guangzhou, China
1 2 3 4 5 6 7 8 9 0 24 23 22 21 20

022020
100919

Project Coordinator: John Willis Art Director: Terry Paulhus

AV2 acknowledges Alamy, Getty, iStock, Minden Pictures, and Shutterstock as the primary image suppliers for this title.